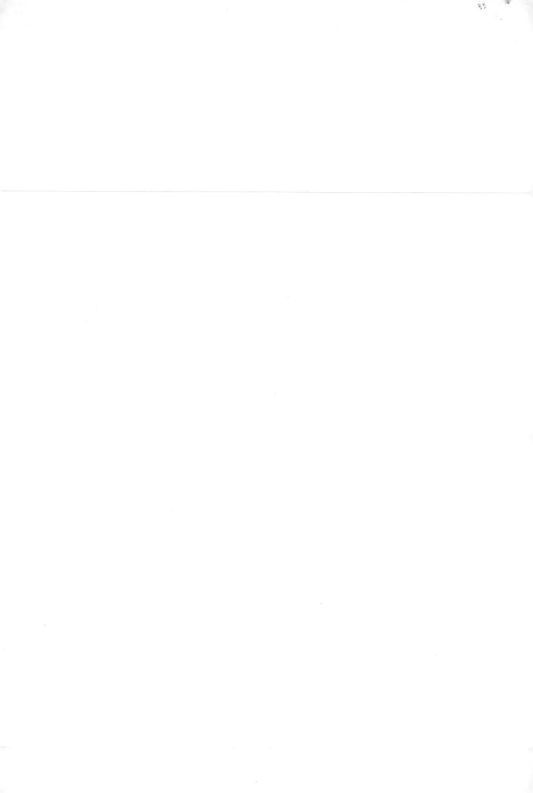

July 4, 1776

The Declaration of American Independence

Brian Williams

A⁺
Smart Apple Media

First published by Cherrytree Press
(a member of the Evans Publishing Group)
327 High Street, Slough
Berkshire SL1 1TX, United Kingdom
Copyright © 2002 Evans Brothers Limited
This edition published under license from
Evans Brothers Limited. All rights reserved.

Designed by Neil Sayer, Edited by Louise John

Published in the United States by
Smart Apple Media
1980 Lookout Drive
North Mankato, MN 56003

U.S. publication copyright © 2003 Smart Apple Media
International copyright reserved in all countries. No part of this book may be
reproduced in any form without written permission from the publisher.
Printed in Hong Kong

Library of Congress Cataloging-in-Publication Data

Williams, Brian, 1943- The declaration of American independence / by Brian Williams.
p. cm. — (Dates with history) Includes index. Summary: A discussion of the events leading
up to the American war for independence from Britain, the revolutionary struggle, the
Declaration of Independence, and the beginning of a new nation.
ISBN 1-58340-211-X
1. United States. Declaration of Independence—Juvenile literature. 2. United States—
Politics and government—1775-1783—Juvenile literature. 3. United States—Politics and
government—1783-1789—Juvenile literature. [1. United States—History—Revolution,
1775-1783. 2. United States—Politics and government—1775-1783. 3. United States—
Politics and government—1783-1789. 4. United States. 5. Declaration of Independence.] I.
Title.

E221 .W63 2002   973.3'13—dc21   2002023100

9 8 7 6 5 4 3 2 1

Picture credits:
Mary Evans Picture Library: 9, 11, 13
Peter Newark's American Pictures: Front cover, 7, 10,
12, 14, 15, 16, 17, 19, 20, 21, 22, 23, 24, 25, 26
Topham Picturepoint: 6, 18, 27

Contents

The Fourth of July

The Fourth of July is the most important national holiday in the United States. On this day every year people across the nation gather for family parties and enjoy the holiday fun. The holiday reminds all Americans of the day the United States came into being, when the Declaration of Independence was adopted on July 4, 1776.

Fireworks over the Statue of Liberty during Fourth of July celebrations.

The Declaration of Independence is written on **parchment**. The writing is in 18th-century longhand script. At the bottom are the signatures of 56 leaders of the 13 colonies. They drew up the Declaration to explain why it was right to end British rule in America.

On July 4, 1776, the Declaration was adopted by representatives of the 13 colonies in America. After years of argument and protest, the War of Independence had begun. The

Declaration set out the **colonists**' beliefs, among them "*that all men are created equal, that they are endowed by their Creator with certain unalienable rights, that among these are Life, Liberty, and the pursuit of Happiness.*" It stated that if Americans were denied those rights by an unjust government, they had the right to rebel.

By 1783, the United States had won its fight to become an independent republic. Americans had set an example for other peoples to follow. The Declaration of Independence is today a treasured historic document, on show at the National Archives in Washington, D.C., and its words inspire freedom-loving peoples everywhere.

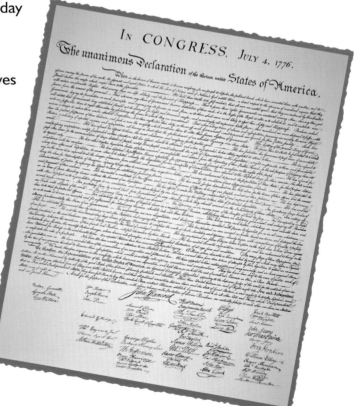

The Declaration of Independence document of July 4, 1776.

British America

In 1776, British America was almost 200 years old. The first colony was set up in 1607 by English **settlers** at Jamestown, Virginia. In 1619 the Virginia colonists started their own government, the House of Burgesses.

Settlers who came from Britain included lords, merchants, soldiers, farmers, and craftworkers. Some

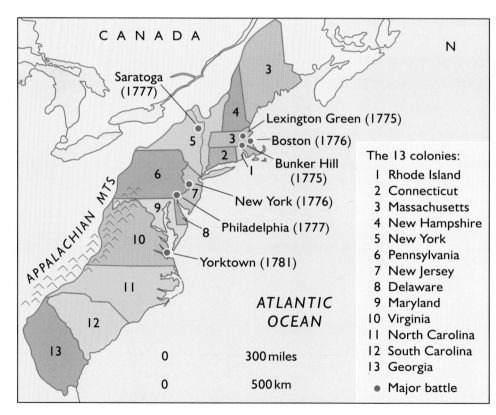

A map of the 13 colonies of British America, showing the major battles of the War of Independence.

A view of the colony of New York, 1750s.

families came to America to find religious freedom. By
1733 there were 13 British colonies on the east coast of
America. Some, like Rhode Island, were small. Others,
like Virginia, were much larger—almost as big as Great
Britain. Land to the north, west, and south was owned
by France and Spain.

Each of the 13 colonies had its own government, but
final power always lay with the governor of each colony,
who was appointed by the British king. The colonists
had to obey laws made by Parliament in Britain.

American society was more free and easy than in Britain.
A few rich people who owned big farms and fine houses
had slaves, but poor people who worked hard could also
prosper. In their new world, Americans looked after
themselves, and they already felt independent.

Protest

France was Britain's rival for control of America. During the French and Indian War of 1754–63, Americans helped British soldiers defeat the French. Victory gave Britain power over much of North America.

The British now had an **empire**, but they had not figured out how to run it. Instead of rewarding the Americans for their help, they demanded higher **taxes** to pay for the war. America was asked to pay for the privilege of being part of the British Empire.

British and French forces in battle during the French and Indian War of 1754–63.

The colonists hated any tax made by a government in which they had no say. They protested, "*No taxation without representation*," pointing out that the London Parliament had no American representatives. The colonists also feared a permanent British army in America, and disliked being asked to house and feed the soldiers. The British government also stopped settlers from moving onto Indian land west of the Appalachian Mountains. To the colonists, this was more interference with their freedoms.

The British government ignored protests, and went ahead with new taxes. The Stamp Act of 1765 forced the colonists to pay tax on printed matter such as newspapers, playing cards, and bills of sale. When they refused to pay, the tax had to be withdrawn.

An example of the stamp that was forced on the colonists in 1765.

In 1767, the British tried again. They put new taxes, or duties, on goods that were shipped into the colonies. So Americans stopped buying British goods, and turned to smuggling to avoid the duties. Some colonists formed secret clubs, called Sons of Liberty, to oppose the new laws.

Reaction

Many Americans hoped the quarrel with Britain would end peacefully. The British still insisted they could make whatever laws they liked for their colonies, and now decided to use force to make their point.

They sent troops into the cities of Boston and New York. The sight of red-coated soldiers on the streets brought out angry crowds. In Boston, on March 5, 1770, British soldiers became scared and fired on a crowd of catcalling citizens. Three people were shot dead, and two later

The Boston Massacre of March 1770.

died of their wounds. Americans called this the "Boston Massacre," and it fueled anti-British feeling.

Britain's next move was to withdraw the hated duties on imported goods—except the one on tea. In 1773, the tax on tea shipped by the British East India Company was cut, making it cheaper than tea shipped from elsewhere. Patriotic Americans hit back by refusing to drink "British" tea. On December 16, 1773, a group of **patriots** dressed as Indians boarded British ships in Boston Harbor and threw chests of tea into the water. This was the "Boston Tea Party."

The Boston Tea Party, 1773.

Now the British government acted tough. It closed the port of Boston and gave the governor of Massachusetts new powers to arrest troublemakers. Angered by these "intolerable" laws, some Americans began to talk openly of a break with Britain.

Colonial leaders met in Philadelphia. Representatives from 12 colonies (all except Georgia) met at the First Continental Congress in September 1774. Some hoped that King George III might help them against an unjust government. He refused to take their side. Any American refusing to obey laws made in London was a rebel.

War

The British government did not know how to deal with America. It fell back on its army. On April 19, 1775, British redcoats clashed with colonial militiamen (part-time soldiers known as "minutemen") at Lexington, Massachusetts. Paul Revere's famous horse ride roused the local people. The British marched on to Concord, where the Americans stopped them. Throughout the colonies, patriots took up weapons. War had begun.

Paul Revere rode his horse to warn local militiamen of the arrival of the British redcoats.

The Second Continental Congress met in May 1775. It set up a Continental Army, and appointed George Washington from Virginia to lead it. The first real battle of the war was fought at Bunker Hill, near Boston, in June 1775. The British lost more than 1,000 soldiers, the Americans about 400.

The Congress sent a last appeal to King George for help, but in August the king told the Americans to end their rebellion or face the consequences. George Washington was hurriedly drilling recruits to face the strong British forces. Fighting spread north into Canada and south into Virginia, where lawyer Patrick Henry made a stirring call to arms: "*Give me liberty or give me death.*"

In January 1776, Thomas Paine published a sensational pamphlet, *Common Sense*. Paine was a recent immigrant to America from England. He argued that Americans could never be free while governed by Britain. Britain was not yet a **democracy**. Americans must bow to the king—or set up a free **republic**.

To many Americans, Paine's words made sense. If they had to fight, it must be for independence. Now was the time to declare the principles for which Americans would fight and die.

The fight at Lexington Common on April 19, 1775.

Jefferson Gets to Work

In June 1776, Richard Henry Lee of Virginia spoke to the Congress. His **resolution** (subject for debate) was *"that these United Colonies are, and of right ought to be, free and independent states."* The Congress set up a five-man committee to draft a Declaration of Independence. The committee members were Thomas Jefferson, Benjamin Franklin, John Adams, Roger Sherman, and Robert Livingston.

Thomas Jefferson drafted the Declaration. He was a lawyer from Virginia, a fast and clearheaded writer. He believed that the Americans had "natural rights," and did not have to obey laws made by the British Parliament, in which they had no say. He set down the reasons why it was right for Americans to govern themselves. He based his arguments on ideas as old as Magna Carta (signed by England's King John in 1215), and on newer principles of

The Declaration Committee members. From left to right: Jefferson, Sherman, Franklin, Livingston, and Adams.

democracy put forward by British philosopher John Locke and French writers Voltaire and Rousseau.

On July 2, the Congress voted to approve Lee's resolution. After discussing Jefferson's draft, on July 4 they voted to adopt it. The document was copied onto parchment. It was then signed by 56 representatives, most doing so on August 2. The first names on the list were John Hancock, president of the Congress, and Charles Thompson, secretary. Hancock wrote his name large to make sure, he said, that King George could read it without eyeglasses.

John Hancock, the first person to sign the Declaration of Independence.

The colonists had taken a historic step. As yet, few Americans had a clear idea of what kind of country or government they were creating. First they had to win the war. If America lost, the men who signed the Declaration of Independence could expect to be hanged as **traitors**.

Who Signed the Declaration?

The colonial leaders who signed the Declaration of Independence were typical of their time. All were men. Women were not yet active in politics, though some American women played a leading part in public life. None were African Americans or Native Americans. Most were well-to-do landowners, "gentlemen" with important positions in the colonies from which they came.

Thomas Jefferson's house in Virginia is now a national monument.

John Hancock, for instance, came from a family of wealthy Boston merchants. John Adams was a lawyer, like Jefferson. Roger Sherman of Connecticut and Robert Livingston of New York were both judges, and another judge, Stephen Hopkins from Rhode Island, had written a pamphlet in 1765 criticizing Britain's rule of its colonies.

Probably the most remarkable of these "Founding Fathers" was Benjamin Franklin. A man of many talents, he had been a printer, publisher, postmaster, scholar, and scientist. One of the first Americans to suggest uniting the American colonies, Franklin had lived for many years in London as an unofficial American **ambassador**. He returned to America in 1775, as the war began, to lend his experience and learning to the Second Continental Congress.

Benjamin Franklin, 1706–93.

The Declaration of Independence expressed the colonists' desire for freedom from what they saw as unjust British rule. They wished to be left alone to govern themselves. Yet few of the leaders were democrats, or shared Thomas Paine's belief in **revolution** and votes for all. Nor, like Paine, did they think of King George as a "royal brute." Each had his own ideas about the kind of nation the United States might be.

19

What the Declaration Said

Britain in the 18th century was governed by its king and by a parliament made up mostly of noblemen and landowners. It was only slowly becoming a **democracy**. Now Americans were declaring their belief in the rights of every citizen to "life, liberty and the pursuit of happiness." What kind of government might this require?

Being a lawyer, Thomas Jefferson knew it was important to make a good case. So the document begins by explaining why Americans had to "throw off" a government that was trying to "reduce them under absolute **despotism**." Despotism was tyranny, and

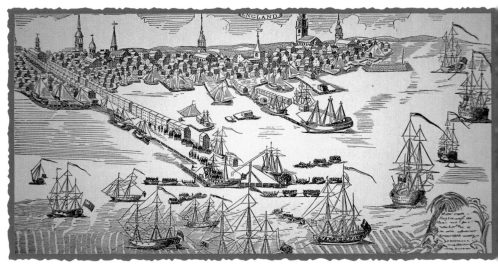

The ships of King George land British troops in Boston, Massachusetts.

absolute despotism was the worst kind. There followed a long list of King George's "crimes." The king was accused of raising unfair taxes, of forcing an unwanted army on America, of waging war with hired troops (Germans) to "complete the works of death, desolation, and tyranny." He had roused black slaves against their masters and was in league with warlike Indians. The king's ships had kidnapped American seamen, "plundered our seas, ravaged our coast, burnt our towns, and destroyed the lives of our people."

Such charges made King George and his government appear far worse than they were. Jefferson was writing to inspire the American people, and to win friends abroad.

George III, king of Great Britain from 1760 to 1820.

The Declaration itself forms the last part of the document. The representatives of the "United States of America," acting "in the name and by authority of the good People of these Colonies," declared that the colonies "are, and of Right ought to be Free and Independent States." The British king and government no longer ruled America.

The Reaction

News of the Declaration was spread by riders galloping along the roads that linked colonial towns. People read about it in newspapers such as the *Boston News-Letter*. Many Americans rejoiced. They banged drums, fired **muskets**, danced on village greens, and raised flags on "liberty-poles."

New Yorkers pull down a statue of King George III to celebrate the Declaration of Independence.

Not all Americans welcomed the Declaration. Some just went on with their daily lives, ignoring the war. A surprisingly large number—about one third of the 3 million people in the colonies—took Britain's side. These people, known as Loyalists, joined the British forces. Many thousands of them moved to Canada or Britain after the war.

Each colony now called itself a state, and set up its own government to replace the king's governor. The running of the war was left to Congress, and to General Washington.

The British government scoffed at the Declaration, though some British politicians such as Charles James Fox supported the Americans. Britain's generals were confident they could beat the Americans easily. Their army of 50,000 soldiers would be too strong for a bunch of colonists with muskets and hunting rifles.

General George Washington, who later became the first president of the United States.

The Americans, however, had several advantages. They were fighting on their home ground. They knew the woods and fields, and could rely on help from civilians. Rather than marching into battle in well-drilled lines, like the redcoats, Americans often fired from the cover of trees and barns. Both sides fought bravely, but American commanders were more daring than the British.

American Victory

The Americans suffered several defeats (they lost New York in 1776 and Philadelphia in 1777). But they always came back, helped by poor British planning. British warships patrolled outside American ports, but failed to cut off America's war supplies. The Americans received help from France, which saw a chance to settle old scores with Britain.

The Americans were fortunate in having George Washington as their general. He had the words of the Declaration read out to every company in his army, so every man knew what he was fighting for.

General Burgoyne surrenders to General Gates at Saratoga, New York, in 1777.

*General Cornwallis surrenders to the Americans at Yorktown
on October 19, 1781.*

In 1777 a British army marched south from Canada, was
cut off, and surrendered to the American general Horatio
Gates at Saratoga, New York. France now joined the war,
and in 1781, the Americans won the final big battle, at
Yorktown, Virginia. Trapped by American and French
forces, General Cornwallis surrendered the last British
army. The Americans had won.

Peace talks began in Paris, France, in 1782. The peace
treaty was signed on September 3, 1783, and Britain finally
recognized the independence of the United States and
agreed on its borders. Now the Americans could truly
celebrate their freedom. The 13 colonies were one nation.

The New Nation

In 1787 the new Constitution of the United States was agreed on by the leaders of the 13 states. Its main authors were Washington, Franklin, James Madison, and Alexander Hamilton. The system they drew up has remained largely unchanged to this day. The Constitution provided three branches of government: the executive (president), the lawmaking body (the two houses of Congress), and the judiciary (the federal courts).

The Americans ended the war victorious, but in debt. One of the first tasks of the new Congress was to pass laws for more taxes. Trade with Britain soon recovered.

George Washington accepts the signed Constitution on September 17, 1787.

In fact, Britain suffered little from its defeat, and learned much. France, on the other hand, was left almost penniless, and this helped bring about the French Revolution of 1789—a revolution inspired by events in America.

In 1789, George Washington was elected the first president of the United States. A Bill of Rights in 1791 guaranteed the rights of every citizen, including freedom of speech, freedom of religion, a free press, and the right to trial by jury.

Thomas Jefferson had dreamed of a democracy of small, independent farmers. This ideal was impractical, as Jefferson found when he became president in 1800. The United States was already too big.

Since the Declaration of Independence, government has become more powerful and complex. The United States has grown from 13 colonies to a union of 50 states, and now ranks as the world's only superpower. Nevertheless, the ideals that lay behind the Declaration remain a

The White House, Washington, D.C.—home of the president of the United States.

strong influence on democratic governments, and on peoples fighting for democracy around the world.

Timeline

1607   First permanent English colony in America, at Jamestown, Virginia.

1619   First colonial government is set up in Virginia.

1643   William Penn founds Pennsylvania, where Philadelphia grows to be colonial America's biggest city.

1763   Britain defeats France for control of North America, and stations troops in the American colonies.

1765   Stamp Act taxes newspapers and legal documents, to the annoyance of Americans.

1770   *March 5:* Three Americans are killed during the "Boston Massacre."

1773   *December 16:* Boston Tea Party is a protest against buying cheap British tea.

1774   Britain gives the governor of Massachusetts new powers and closes Boston port.

1774   *September 5:* First Continental Congress meets at Philadelphia.

1775   *April 19:* Shots fired at Lexington and Concord, beginning the Revolutionary War.

1775   *May 10:* Second Continental Congress meets in Philadelphia.

1775	*June 14:* Congress sets up the Continental Army, and the next day appoints George Washington to command it.
1775	*July:* Congress asks King George III to settle Americans' grievances.
1775	*August 23:* King George III declares the colonists are rebels.
1776	*January:* Tom Paine's pamphlet *Common Sense* argues for American independence.
1776	*June 7:* Richard Henry Lee of Virginia asks Congress to vote for independence.
1776	*July 2:* Congress votes "yes" to Lee's resolution.
1776	*July 4:* Congress adopts the final draft of the Declaration of Independence.
1776	*August 2:* John Hancock and other leaders sign the Declaration.
1780	French troops land to help the Americans.
1781	*October 19:* At Yorktown, Virginia, British army surrenders.
1782	*April:* Peace talks begin in Paris, France.
1783	*September 3:* The Treaty of Paris officially ends the war. Britain recognizes the independent United States.
1787	The Constitution of the United States is agreed on.
1789	George Washington is elected the first president of the United States.

Glossary

ambassador The official representative of one country in another country, heading an embassy.

colonists A group of people who move from their own country to start a settlement (a colony) in another land.

democracy System of government controlled by the people, through an elected lawmaking assembly.

despotism Rule by a person who does what he or she likes, sharing power with no one and behaving as a tyrant.

empire A group of nations or peoples under the rule of a single person or government.

musket Long gun fired from the shoulder, like a rifle, used in the 18th century.

parchment An old-fashioned type of paper, made from animal skin.

patriot Person who loves his or her country enough to work and fight for it.

republic Democratic form of government, run by elected officials and often headed by a president, as in the U.S.A.

resolution A statement or decision to be discussed and debated by a group of people, who then vote for or against.

revolution Violent overthrow of a ruler or government.

settlers People who make their homes in a new land, often far from home.

taxes Money people have to pay to the government. Duties are taxes charged on things people buy and sell.

traitor Person who acts against his or her country's government or ruler.

Index